CLEVER CRAFTS for Kids

Annalees Lim

WAYLAND

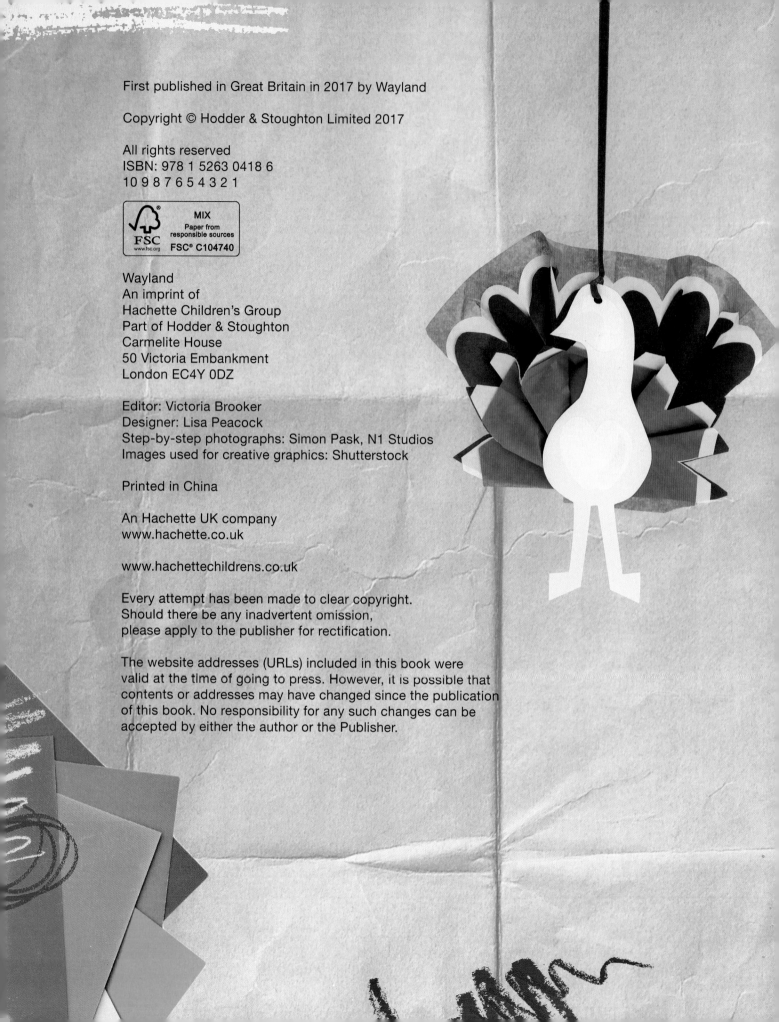

First published in Great Britain in 2017 by Wayland

Copyright © Hodder & Stoughton Limited 2017

FSC
MIX
Paper from
responsible sources
www.fsc.org FSC® C104740

Wayland
An imprint of
Hachette Children's Group
Part of Hodder & Stoughton
Carmelite House
50 Victoria Embankment
London EC4Y 0DZ

Editor: Victoria Brooker
Designer: Lisa Peacock
Step-by-step photographs: Simon Pask, N1 Studios
Images used for creative graphics: Shutterstock

Printed in China

An Hachette UK company
www.hachette.co.uk

www.hachettechildrens.co.uk

Contents

crafts made with FABRIC

Contents

Fun with Fabric

If you think having fun with fabric means sewing and stitching, think again! There is so much you can make with material, felt, buttons and wool without even threading a needle.

Small scraps of fabric, spare beads and buttons can be easily found around your home. It is a good idea to keep them all together so when you are in the mood to make something, you can find them easily. Try storing them in an old shoebox and decorate it in a similar way to the books on page 16.

To keep your crafts nice and clean, always work in a clear area and put down a table covering first, especially if you are using glue. Material is a little harder to cut with scissors than paper so ask an adult for help.

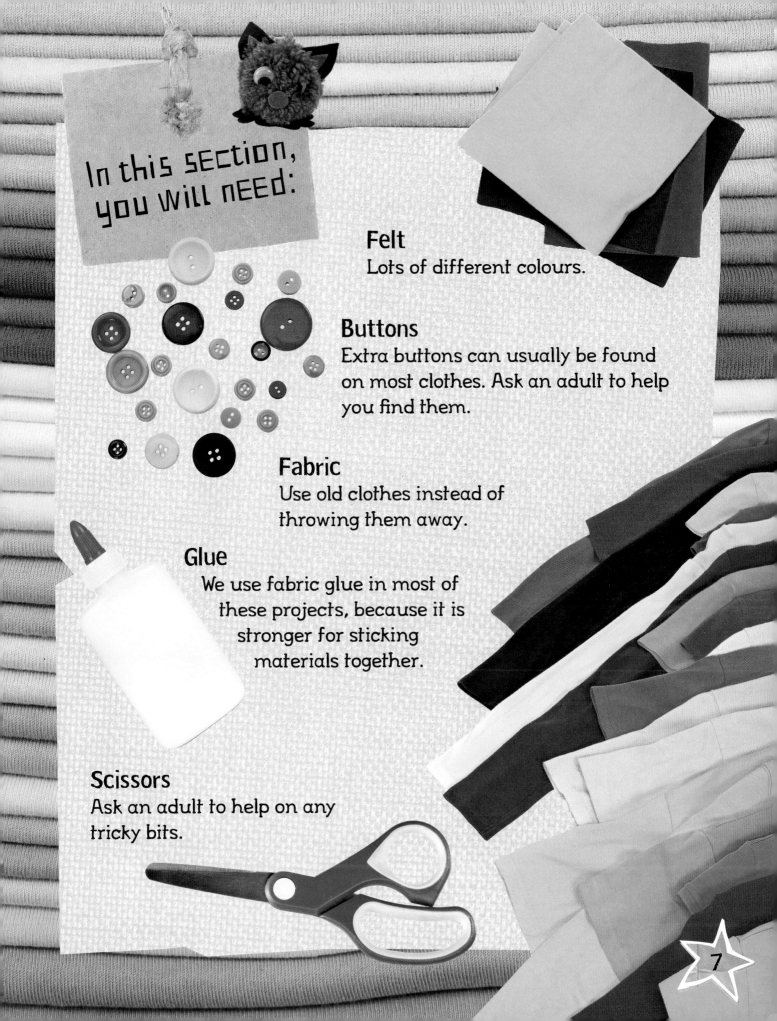

In this section, you will need:

Felt
Lots of different colours.

Buttons
Extra buttons can usually be found on most clothes. Ask an adult to help you find them.

Fabric
Use old clothes instead of throwing them away.

Glue
We use fabric glue in most of these projects, because it is stronger for sticking materials together.

Scissors
Ask an adult to help on any tricky bits.

Finger Puppet Kingdom

Create a kingdom at your fingertips full of kings, queens, princes and princesses, protected by brave knights.

You will need:
Scrap paper or card
Pen
Different coloured felt
Fabric glue
Scissors

1

Draw your finger puppet template onto a piece of scrap paper and cut out.

2

Use the template to draw onto two pieces of felt. Cut out these shapes.

3

Glue the shapes together leaving the flat edge open so that your finger can be placed inside.

4

Cut out two circles for hands, two ear shapes and two eyes.

5

Once you have made one finger puppet you can make any character you can think of. If you are stuck for inspiration, think of your favourite story or nursery rhyme.

Make a king by cutting out a crown, red robes, hair and a moustache. You can cut out different shapes to make the rest of the puppets!

Fun Felt Veggie Patch

You will need:
Different coloured felt
Scissors
Glue
Wooden stick
Plastic pot
Googly eyes

You don't have to be an expert gardener to create your very own vegetable patch. These fun veggies are simple to make and even easier to keep!

1

To make peas in a pod, cut out a green ellipse shape and two thin curved shapes

2

Glue the wooden stick onto the middle of the green ellipse.

3

Cut out three light green peas and glue to cover the stick.

4

Glue the curved shapes onto the edge of the ellipse, covering the sides of the peas.

5

Glue the eyes onto the peas and leave to dry. Use the same technique to make more veggies. Roll some scrap felt into a pot to stand your veggies in.

Vegetables aren't the only things that can thrive in your soil patch. Try making felt flowers or felt fruit to plant!

Plaited Pals

You will need:
Fabric
Scissors
Wool
Glue
Googly eyes

Create these funky fabric snail friends with just some scrap material, wool and a set of fun googly eyes.

1

Cut three pieces of fabric to the same width and length.

2

Tie the three lengths together with a knot.

3

Cut the short ends in two and wrap each section with wool to make antennae.

4

Plait the long lengths together.

Try making a lovely, spotty ladybird or a creeping, crawling spider with this plaited pals technique.

5

Roll the plaited end up until it reaches the top and glue in place. Glue some googly eyes onto the knot to make your snail's face.

Woven Art

You will need:

- A4 size thick card
- Wool
- Scraps of material
- Scissors
- A4 black card

Have fun making this stunning woven art panel that looks great hung up on any wall.

1

Cut triangle grooves out of the short ends of the thick card.

2

Wind the wool around the card using the grooves as a guide. When you have covered the card tie both ends of the wool together to secure it.

Weave scraps of fabric in and out of the wool until the whole board is full.

You can make many of these small woven panels, carefully remove them from the card loom and sew them together to make a cool rug or blanket for your bed.

Trim any long ends to neaten the weaving.

Fold the black card in half and cut a heart shape. Open the cut card out and glue this on top of your weaving to frame your piece of art.

Felt Pattern Book Cover

You will need:
A book to decorate
Different coloured felt
Scissors
Googly eyes
Fabric glue

Decorate your old notepads or exercise books with these fancy felt figures.

Your felt friends can be stuck onto nearly any surface by using your fabric glue. Try sticking them to bags, keepsake boxes or school folders.

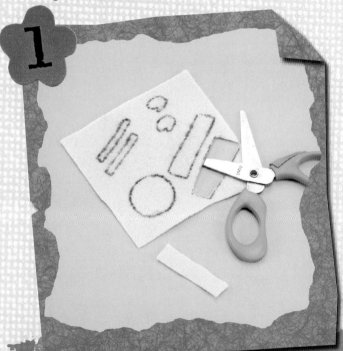

1

Cut a head, two arms, two legs and two hands out of some felt.

2

Cut a t-shirt out of white felt and cut out red lines to make the pirate stripes and red shoes and a pirate hat.

3

Cut out some brown shorts, a black eye patch and a silver sword.

4

Glue all the pieces onto the book using fabric glue and finish off the face with the black eye patch and a googly eye.

5

Surround your pirate with some yellow stars. You could create different felt characters for some other books.

Sock Monsters

You will need:
Old socks
Cushion stuffing
Pipe cleaners
Googly eyes
Fabric glue

Shape and mould your very own mini monsters out of old socks and pipe cleaners!

1

Stuff your old, but clean, sock with the cushion stuffing until it is nearly full.

Mini monsters can be made from any items of clothing you are about to throw out. Cut off sleeves from an old jumper and sew up one end, or stuff an old woolly glove.

2

Poke the open end inside your sock to keep the stuffing secure.

3

Tie a pipe cleaner around its middle to create a head. Glue two googly eyes of different sizes onto the head using some fabric glue.

4

Carefully cut two holes at the top of the head. Push a pipe cleaner through them to make some antennae.

5

Cut small holes either side of the sock monster. Cut a pipe cleaner in half and push a half through each side to make some arms.

Button Buddies

You will need:
- Elastic
- Measuring tape
- Scissors
- Buttons

Don't let the spare buttons you have lying around and hidden in drawers go to waste! Build your very own button buddy that you can carry around with you or hang on your bag.

1

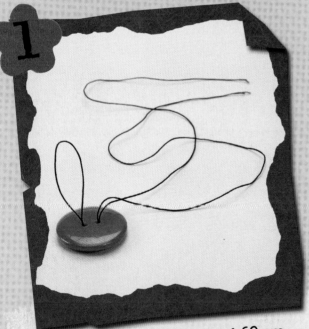

Cut a piece of elastic about 60 cm long and fold in half. Thread the folded end through the holes of a large button and tape in place.

2

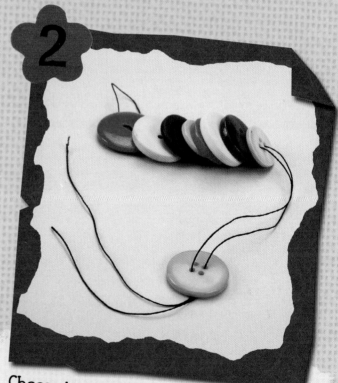

Choose ten buttons for the body and thread them on to the elastic.

Thread about 12 buttons onto each strand to make the legs. Tie a knot to secure in place.

Try making your buddies with different sizes and colours of buttons. You can take buttons from old clothes, but remember to ask an adult beforehand.

Cut a piece of elastic about 30 cm long. Thread about 20 buttons onto this. Tie at the ends and then tie it beneath the head to make the arms.

Glue some googly eyes onto the head to bring your button buddy to life!

21

Pom Pom Pals

You will need:
Compass and pencil
Card
Scissors
Wool
Googly eyes
Felt
Fabric glue

Create cute pom pom pals for you and your friends using scrap wool and some felt.

1 Use your compass to draw two large circles of the same size onto some card. Draw a smaller circle on each and cut out.

2 Place these two rings together. Tie some wool onto the circle and loop the wool around it. Keep winding until you have at least three layers.

3

Cut though the wool in between the two rings. Slide some wool between the card and tie a knot. Remove the card rings.

4

Glue googly eyes onto the pom pom. Cut some feet and a nose out of some felt and glue these on.

Don't worry if you don't have a whole ball of wool to use. Pom pom pals can be made using scrap pieces of wool to make a multicoloured pom pom pal!

5

Make some ears out of felt and stick them to the top of the pom pom with fabric glue.

PetPouches

Keep your treasures safe with a pet pouch. Decorate these simple drawstring pouches with your favourite animal.

1

With the fabric facing the right side towards you, put glue down one side and the bottom. Fold in half, press together and leave to dry.

Make these pouches any size you like. Small pouches can be used to store jewellery or as party bags and bigger pouches can be used as a book bag.

2

Turn the material inside out so that the right side is on the outside. Fold down 2 cm of material from the top. Cut two triangles 2 cm from the edge.

3

Cut some features out of felt to make your animal. For a rabbit, you will need two ears, cheeks, whiskers, a nose and teeth.

4

Glue the felt onto the pouch with fabric glue. Add some googly eyes.

5

Thread the ribbon in and out of the holes at the top of the pouch, and pull together. Tie the ribbon in a bow to secure the pouch.

natural
CRAFTS

Contents

Fun with Nature

You can have lots of fun with nature! You just have to step outside and look around you. Collect stones, shells, twigs and leaves when you're out and about to make fantastic pieces of art.

Be inspired by the natural world that you pass by every day. Notice the trees changing through the seasons from young, green shoots emerging in spring to the red and brown leaves falling in autumn. Every season there are new materials for you to use!

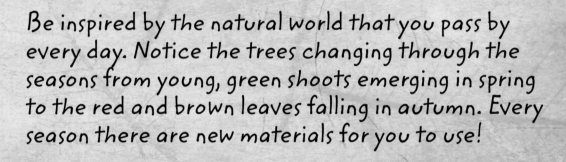

Always ask a grown up before you pick anything up. Lots of things should stay where you find them. A good rule is to only collect what has fallen from plants or trees and never pick anything that is still alive or growing. Remember to wash your findings before you use them.

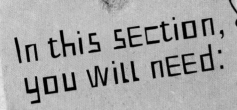

Paint and paintbrushes

To decorate your crafts.
Use poster paints or
acrylic paints.

Paper or card

To display or decorate
your crafts.

Clay

Air-drying clay can be found in
most craft shops and even in some
larger supermarkets.

Glue

PVA is a really strong glue used to stick
different materials together. If you are gluing
any fabric remember to use fabric glue.

Scissors

Use child-size scissors. Ask an adult to help
where suggested, or on any tricky bits.

Mini-Greenhouse Planter

You will need:
One 2-litre drink bottle
Scissors
White electrical tape or masking tape
Plastic food tray or plant pot base
Card
Sticky tape
Soil
Seeds

Nurture small seeds into little plants before you pot them outside with this indoor greenhouse! All you need is a plastic bottle, a base, some soil and some seeds.

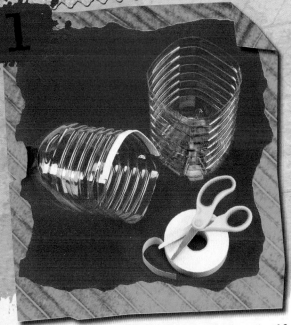

1

Ask an adult to cut the bottle in half. You will only need the top half for this project. Put masking tape around the cut edge to make it less sharp.

2

Using the tape, create the lines of your greenhouse, starting with the walls and roof.

There is no need to throw away the left-over plastic bottle. Try covering it in papier-mâché, leaving it to dry and then painting it to create a handy pencil pot!

3

Make windows and a door with the tape.

4

Cut some green card into the shape of grass. Stick this green card to the plastic tray.

5

Fill the plastic tray with soil and plant your seeds. Cover the seeds with the plastic greenhouse and leave to grow, watering occasionally.

Leafy Print Wrapping Paper

You will need:
Leaves
Large piece of paper
Paint
Paintbrush

Create your own unique wrapping paper all year round by using leaves you have collected from the garden or a walk in the park.

1

Choose a selection of leaves that are different shapes and sizes.

2

Paint a thin layer of paint onto one of the leaves. Remember to do this on top of a piece of scrap paper so you don't make a mess!

3

Place the painted side of your leaf onto your large piece of paper and press down lightly to create a print.

4

Repeat with different colours and leaf shapes until the whole piece of paper is covered. Leave to dry before you wrap your present!

Make your wrapping paper extra special by adding some glitter glue to the outside of the leaves to make them sparkle. Try printing onto coloured paper or even brown parcel paper!

Seashell Clay Prints

You will need:
- Air-drying clay
- Rolling pin
- A collection of seashells
- Paint
- Paintbrush
- Pencil
- Wool or string

Make use of any seashells you find on holiday by creating a decorative clay print. Perfect to hang in your room and remind you of lovely times you had at the seaside!

1

Roll out the air-drying clay until it is about 2 cm thick.

2

Using a card template that is about 10 cm x 10 cm, cut a square shape out of the clay using an old butter knife.

3

Choose your favourite seashells and gently press them into the soft clay to make prints.

4

Use the handle of a paint brush to make two holes at the top of the tile. Leave to dry in a dry warm place for about 1–2 days.

5

Once the whole tile is completely dry, decorate using acrylic paints. Leave to dry and thread some wool through the holes to hang it up!

Pine Cone Hedgehog Family

Make your own hedgehog family using pine cones that you can find on a woodland walk!

You will need:

Pine cones
Plasticine or clay
Paint brush
Sharp pencil

1

Using some beige coloured clay, mould a cone shape for the face, two flat discs for ears and four small balls for the feet.

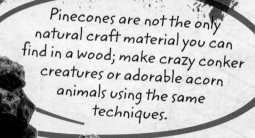

Pinecones are not the only natural craft material you can find in a wood; make crazy conker creatures or adorable acorn animals using the same techniques.

2

Press the cone onto the flat end of the pine cone until it is stuck firmly in place. Next press the ears on top. Use the handle of a paintbrush to make a dip in each ear.

3

Use the handle of the paintbrush again to create two holes for the eyes. Carefully use a sharp pencil to create a slit for the mouth.

4

Turn the hedgehog over and press the four balls onto the bottom of the pine cone to make the feet.

5

Mould two white and two blue balls for the eyes. Fill the holes you made in the cone-shape face with these balls. Your first family member is ready; now you can make more!

Dried Flower Field

You will need:

Flowers
Kitchen paper
Heavy books
A4 sheet of blue card
Green, yellow and white paper
Green tissue paper
Scissors
Glue

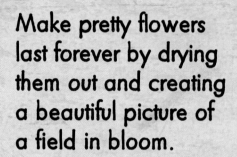

Make pretty flowers last forever by drying them out and creating a beautiful picture of a field in bloom.

1

Place a selection of flowers between two sheets of kitchen paper and place these between two heavy books. Leave for four weeks to dry out.

2

When the flowers are ready, cut some clouds out of white paper and a wavy shape out of green paper to make rolling hills.

3

Cut out a circle from some yellow paper and some long triangles to make the sun's rays.

You could use your dried flowers for many craft projects. Make a picture of a vase of flowers or glue them onto a box to make a lovely birthday gift.

4

Cut out some stems and leaves for the flowers from the green tissue paper.

5

Glue all of the paper pieces onto the blue card. Then glue the dried flowers onto the green stems. Your picture is complete!

Mini Forest

You will need:

Twigs
String
Plastic yoghurt pot
Stones or pebbles
Green tissue paper
Glue
Scissors

Create your very own enchanted forest inside your house from sticks you've collected from your garden, park or a walk in the woods.

Who could live in your forest? Maybe you could draw and cut out people to wander through the trees or use it as a home for the hedgehog family you can make on pages 36-37.

1

Gather some twigs into a bundle. Tie them together with string.

2

Place the twigs in the yoghurt pot and fill it with the small stones so that the miniature tree can stand on its own.

3

Cut out small leaf shapes from the tissue paper. You can decide whether you want spring green trees, red and orange trees for autumn, or a multicoloured magical forest using blues and purple.

4

Glue the leaves onto the ends of the twigs to make full branches. Now make some more to fill your forest.

Stone Painting

You will need:
Stones, pebbles and rocks
Paint
Paintbrush
PVA glue
Googly eyes
White felt
Scissors

Create many colourful creatures by painting rocks, pebbles or stones. These buzzing bees make great ornaments, colourful bookends or pretty paper weights.

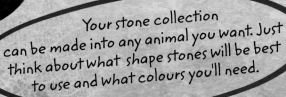
Your stone collection can be made into any animal you want. Just think about what shape stones will be best to use and what colours you'll need.

1

Choose a stone and paint it yellow. Leave to dry in a warm place.

2

Once the yellow paint is dry, paint three thick black stripes onto the stone.

3

Using PVA glue, stick two googly eyes onto the front of the stone.

4

Cut out some wings from the white felt. Glue on to the top of the stone and leave to dry completely.

Nature Family Portraits

You will need:

Leaves
Coloured and white paper
Magazines
Scissors
PVA glue
Black felt-tip pen

Create crazy family portraits using leaves and other craft materials.

If you want your family portraits to look exactly like the members of your family, take a photograph and print them out. You can then cut out their features and stick them onto the leafy head and bodies.

1

Glue a leaf onto a coloured piece of paper. This will make the head of your portrait.

2

Cut out eyes, noses, mouths, ears and hair from different people in an old magazine. Choose some and glue in place on the leaf.

3

Once the glue is dry, cut out the head leaving a small border of coloured paper.

4

Glue this onto the white paper. Draw some arms and legs to create your person. Make lots of people and glue them onto the same page to make a family!

Nature Crown

If you have made too many leaves or twig triangles, try gluing them onto lengths of string to make a cool hanging for your window.

You will need:

Twigs
PVA glue
Paint or glue brush
Leaves
Tissue paper
Gold card
Stapler
Plastic pocket

Be the king or queen of the forest with this spectacular nature crown.

1

Cut the tissue paper into rectangles. Paint with glue. Lay three twigs on top in a triangle shape. Fold the tissue paper over the twigs and paint on more glue. Make about six triangles and leave to dry.

2

On a plastic pocket, cover a sheet of tissue paper in PVA glue. The plastic pocket makes the tissue paper easier to peel off when dry. Stick some leaves onto the sheet. Make two of these sheets in different colours.

3

Once the sheets are dry, cut the leaves out keeping a coloured border around them.

4

Staple strips of gold card together to make a crown that will fit onto your head.

5

Use sticky tape or glue to attach the triangles and leaves to complete your crown.

crafts using PAINT

Contents

Fun with Paint

You can have lots of fun with paint. In this section, you can paint with your fingers, with cotton buds and with scrunched up paper. You can even add different textures to the paint such as rice or oats.

You can also mix paints. Did you know that with just three colours, red, blue and yellow, you can create a whole range of colours. These are called the three primary colours and by mixing them in different combinations, you can make any colour you want!

Before you start painting, always cover surfaces with newspaper so it's easy to clear up any spills. Put on an apron or an old top. Find a space where you can leave your projects to dry. Then you're ready to paint!

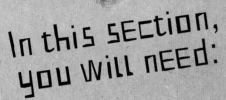

In this section, you will need:

Paint
Poster paints or acrylic paints are best for these projects.

Paintbrushes
It's good to have a few different-sized paintbrushes. Remember always to clean your paintbrush after you've finished your craft.

Coloured card or paper
To make your pictures and crafts with. You don't have to use the colours suggested in this book.

Glue
PVA is great for mixing into paint to make it stronger. Glue sticks are useful for sticking pictures to card to make frames.

Scissors
Use child-size scissors. Ask an adult to help you with any tricky bits.

Mixing pallet
To hold the paint and to mix different colours. You could use a lid from an old plastic container.

Colour Wheel

You will need:
Thin card
Compass
Pencil
Scissors
Ruler
Red, blue and yellow paint
Paintbrush
Mixing pallet

You can have lots of fun with paint, but do you know what colours go well with others? Make this handy wheel to help you make great colour choices and learn how to mix colours.

1

Draw a large circle on the card with your compass. Cut out the circle.

2

Draw a line through the middle and then across to create four equal quarters. Divide each quarter into three to make 12 sections.

3

Paint a primary colour (red, blue and yellow) in each third of the circle, making sure there are three blank sections between each one.

4

Paint your secondary colours (purple, orange and green) next. For purple, mix blue and red. For orange, mix red and yellow. For green, mix yellow and blue.

Colours directly opposite each other on the colour wheel are contrasting colours. This means they go well with each other. Colours that are beside each other on the colour wheel are complimentary colours and work in harmony with each other.

5

For the tertiary colours, mix whatever colours are either side of the blank section you want to fill. For example, mix primary yellow and secondary green to make light green.

Handy Farmyard

Create a whole farmyard full of animals just by using your hands. First learn to print a whole flock of clucking chickens, and when you get the hang of it there are lots more animals you can try your hand at!

Fill your farmyard: Try printing a cow with horns and hoofs; a peacock with long feathers; a sitting duck with a beak and wings; or a sheep with a fluffy coat and tail.

You will need:
Paint
Paintbrush
White paper
Coloured paper
Black felt-tip pen
Glue

1

Paint you whole hand any colour you like.

2

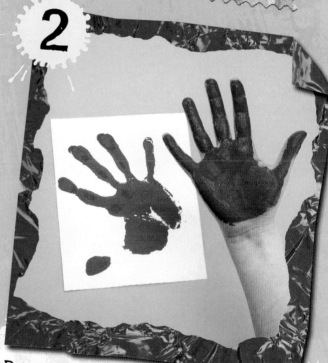

Print your hand onto a white piece of paper and leave to dry. Then wash your hand.

3

Use a black pen to draw the outline of your chicken, using the handprint as a guide. Start drawing a head with a beak and wattle on the thumb. Then add the body, tail and feet.

4

Cut out your handprint chicken and glue it to a coloured background. Try a green piece of paper to look like grass. Now try a different animal!

Wax Crayon Batik Owl

You will need:
A pale coloured crayon
White paper
Watered-down paint or watercolours
Cotton bud
Coloured paper
Scissors
Glue

Batik was used by the ancient Egyptians. You can have a go too, with this simple method using just your wax crayons and some watery paint.

2 Mix some watery paints in your pallet. Paint over the whole page. Use different shades and blend them with water.

1 Draw a picture of an owl with your crayon. You could copy the one above or copy one from a book.

Use the same technique to send secret notes to friends. Write your note in crayon and ask your friend to paint over to reveal what you've said!

3

Before the paint completely dries use the cotton bud to wipe off the paint from the wax crayon lines. This will make the lines really bright.

4

Make a frame for your picture by folding a piece of card in half and cutting out the middle. Make the sides uneven to make it look like the owl is poking out through leaves.

5

Glue the frame on top of your owl. Your owl picture is now ready to hang in your bedroom!

Dotty about Fireworks

You will need:
Paint
Black paper or card
Cotton buds
Grey paper or card
Scissors
Pencil
Ruler
Glue

Watch fireworks whizzing and banging in a starry sky all year round by painting your own scene. You could make them really sparkle and shimmer by sprinkling the wet paint with glitter.

Paint a red firework in the middle of the black card using a cotton bud to make the dots.

Paint two more fireworks in different colours either side using the same technique.

3

Paint bright yellow bursts of dots in the centre of each firework and white dots on the outside. Leave to dry.

4

Draw a skyline onto the grey paper and cut out.

5

Glue the skyline onto the bottom of the black card. Your picture is ready to display!

Scrunched Seascape

You will need:
White paper
Paint
Scrunched-up newspaper
  or tissue paper
Scissors
Glue

Painting waves and sunny skies can take a while to learn, but with this simple technique you can create a fantastic seascape that will make you look like a master painter!

All sorts of shapes can be cut out of the stippled paper to create different scenes.

1

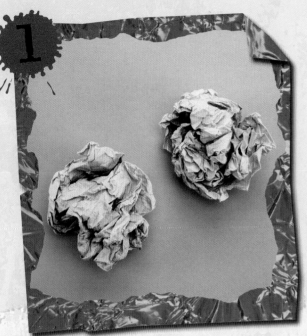

Scrunch up old bits of tissue paper into small balls.

2

Dunk the balls in paint and stamp them lightly all over a blank piece of paper. Make lots of sheets using different colours of paint.

3

Once the paper is dry, cut into shapes that will make your seascape. You will need some waves, a beach, a sun and a palm tree.

4

Stick your shapes onto a blue painted background. Try making different scenes using this technique.

Snowflake Wrapping Paper

Stencils are a quick and easy way to make repeat patterns and add a bit of colour to any plain bits of paper. The stencils are also really fun to make and, just like real snowflakes, they come out differently each time!

1

Fold a piece of paper in half, then quarters and then fold in half again to make a triangle shape.

2

Trim the top so it looks like an ice cream cone in shape.

3

Cut shapes into the sides and top. Open it up to reveal your snowflake stencil.

You could make the wrapping paper extra special by dabbing glue on and then sprinkling glitter on top.

4

Place the snowflake on a large piece of paper and dab paint through the holes of the stencil. Cover your whole piece of paper with snowflakes.

3-D Rainbow

Mix together this gloopy paint recipe to create a beautiful rainbow that really stands out from the page.

You will need:

Mixing pot
Paint
PVA glue
Porridge oats, rice, sugar
  or pencil sharpenings
Compass
Pencil
Paper
Shiny or sparkly paper

1

In a pot, mix 1 part glue to 3 parts paint. Add your chosen texture (oats, rice, sugar or sharpenings) and mix well. Make four of these mixtures in different colours.

2

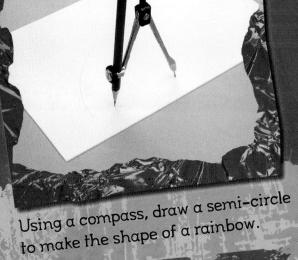

Using a compass, draw a semi-circle to make the shape of a rainbow.

Try using the same technique to create wavy waves in a seascape or give people funky hairstyles on top of faces you have painted.

3

Paint a thick line of textured paint onto the semi-circle. Paint another line underneath and so on to create your rainbow.

4

Cut out shiny clouds and rain and glue on to the picture to make your scene complete.

River Reflections

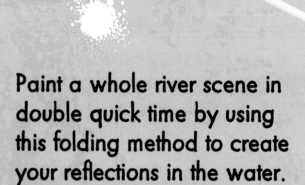

Paint a whole river scene in double quick time by using this folding method to create your reflections in the water.

1

Fold a piece of pale blue paper in half, long ways.

2

Paint the bottom half in a darker shade of blue. Use watery paint so that it looks more like a river.

66

You can print other reflections too. Try palm trees in a desert oasis or tall city buildings that are beside a wide river.

3

Paint a landscape on the top half of the paper full of trees, bushes and flowers.

4

Fold the paper in half and press firmly. Open up carefully to reveal your river reflection!

Foil Prints

Kitchen foil that you find in your kitchen cupboards is not only useful when baking or cooking, it is a great craft material that you can use to make fantastic repeat patterns.

1

Cut a large piece of kitchen foil and fold it in half.

Try drawing the letters of your name to make a simple bedroom sign. Just remember to write everything backwards so it prints the right way round!

2

Using a blunt pencil, draw an outline of a house. Press firmly so that it makes a deep dent. This is easier to do if you lean on a stack of magazines or paper.

3

Cover the drawing with a thin layer of paint.

4

Place the foil print on top of your blank card or folded paper and press firmly.

5

Carefully peel of the foil print. Your card print is ready to send. Try different pictures and colours.

crafts made with PAPER

Contents

Fun with Paper

You can find paper everywhere in different sizes, shapes, colours and textures. From coloured paper to newspaper, tissue paper to wrapping paper, paper can be found all around your home.

Transforming your piece of paper is easy. In this section, you will learn how to decorate paper using paints and felt-tip pens; join paper with glue, sticky tape and staples; and shape your paper by folding, tearing and cutting.

Paper is the perfect material to be creative with. Once you learn the basics, there is no end to the paper crafts you can make. Try adapting the projects in this section using different designs, colours or by adding glitter and sparkles.

Wrapping paper

Torn paper

Newspaper

In this section, you will need:

Felt-tip pens
Any shape or thickness. You don't have to follow the colours used in this book.

Paint
To decorate your crafts. Use poster paints or acrylic paints.

Paintbrushes
It's good to have a few different-sized paintbrushes. Always clean your paintbrush when you've finished.

Glue
We use PVA glue in most of these projects, because it is strong and easy to apply.

Scissors
Use child-size scissors. Ask an adult to help you with any tricky bits.

Ribbon, string or cotton
To hang up your decorations. Any colour will do.

73

Paper Pet Chains

You will need:

Paper approx. 60 cm x 10 cm
Ruler
Pencil
Scissors
Felt-tip pens
Scrap pieces of coloured paper,
glitter and glue to decorate

Decorate your room with these cute paper pals. You can use your own pet as inspiration, or dream up a new creature to hang on your walls.

1

Fold the piece of paper backwards and forwards into a concertina shape, making sure that the folds are 10 cm wide.

2

Draw the picture of your pet on the top fold. The picture must touch both sides of the paper. This will make sure that all the pets are linked together.

Paper chains aren't just great for your bedroom, they are also a fantastic way to decorate a room for parties. Just draw a picture that matches the theme and cut out to create the perfect party paper chains.

3

Cut out the shape using scissors and open out. Do not cut along where the picture touches the edges. These points will hold the chain together.

4

Decorate each pet shape using your colouring pens, glitter or cut out pieces of paper. You can make each one the same, or all different.

Animal Masks

Go wild with this lion mask! But don't stop there – why not make a happy hippo or an exotic bird of paradise?

You will need:
Orange and yellow paper plates
Scissors
Blu tack or plasticine
A sharp pencil
Glue
Tissue paper
Colouring pens
Hole punch
String or elastic

Cut the yellow plate in half. In one half, cut out a small 'n' shape in the middle of the flat side to fit around your nose. Use the other half to cut out two ears and a nose.

Put blu tack under the plate where you want eyeholes. Carefully push a sharp pencil through the paper plate into the blu tack. Ask an adult to cut an eye shape. Repeat to make the other eye.

Cut the orange plate into eight segments. Glue these orange pieces around the yellow plate to make the mane. Then glue the yellow ears and nose on.

Cut slits into a length of tissue paper to make some extra mane. Glue this behind the paper mane. Draw around the edges with colouring pens to make the features stand out.

Use your hole punch to make holes at the side of the mask. Tie string or elastic on and it's ready to wear!

77

Concertina Butterflies

You will need:
Coloured card
Pen
Scissors
6 sheets of A4-sized tissue paper
Stapler
Sticky tape
Hole punch
Coloured ribbon or string

Make fluttering butterflies, soaring birds, and other fun flying creatures to hang from your ceiling. We will be making a beautiful butterfly, but you can use the same technique to make any winged creature you can think of!

Draw the shape of a butterfly's body onto the coloured card and cut out.

Lay three pieces of tissue paper on top of each other and fold them backwards and forwards as if you were making a fan. Repeat with the other three pieces of tissue.

3

Cut the folded bits of tissue paper in two to make four pieces. Make sure that four pieces are longer than the other two.

4

Fan out each tissue paper piece and staple in place on the card butterfly body.

5

Cut out another piece of card, slightly smaller than the butterfly body, and glue on top of the pink body. Make a hole in the top of the head using the hole punch. Tie some ribbon through the hole and hang your butterfly up.

Robot Weaving

Make a robot with a colourful circuit board tummy by weaving with coloured pieces of paper. You can make your robots different shapes and sizes – just use your imagination to create a fantastic team of robots.

You will need:
A4 grey card
Black pen
Scissors
Ruler
Coloured paper cut into
1 cm-wide strips

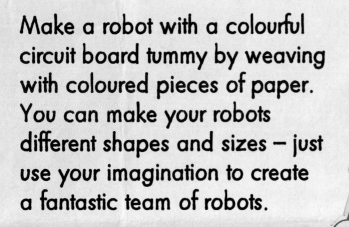

Fold the card in half, lengthways, and draw half a robot. Draw one leg, one arm, half a body and half a head as shown above.

Cut out the shape of the robot and keep it folded in half.

Using your ruler, draw lines on the body of your robot that are about 1 cm apart. Cut along the lines.

Open out the robot. Weave the coloured lengths of paper in and out of the slits you have cut. Switch from starting under to over for each slit.

Cut the ends of the coloured paper strips so they don't show. Draw on the details of your robot with the black pen.

Mosaic Minibeasts

You will need:
- Scraps of paper
- Scissors
- Ruler
- Glue
- A4 white paper
- Pencil
- A4 black card
- Black pen

You don't need to travel to ancient Rome to enjoy mosaics. Make your own using any paper you can find and cutting it into small squares. Recycle scraps of wrapping paper, old birthday cards or magazines to create your minibeast masterpiece.

1

Cut the pieces of scrap paper into 2 cm-wide strips and then cut each strip into small squares that are roughly the same size.

2

Stick the squares of coloured paper onto the white A4 paper leaving a small gap between each square.

82

You can use your mosaic minibeasts to decorate almost anything. Stick them on notebooks, cards or mount them in a frame.

4

3

Make a stencil by drawing a flower shape on a piece of paper. Cut it out and draw around it two times on the mosaic.

Cut the shapes out. Repeat all the steps to make more mosaics for your minibeasts scene. You will need some leaves, a caterpillar, butterfly and dragonfly. Stick all of these onto the black piece of card.

83

Stapled Paper Hearts

These lovely decorations are perfect to make and hang in your window. You could use sparkly paper to make them really catch the light.

Try using smaller pieces of paper to make mini versions. They are perfect to use as fancy gift tags.

You will need:
Coloured paper
Scissors
Stapler
Cotton or string
Sticky tape

1

Cut four strips of paper the same width but different lengths. Make sure they are in height order. Staple them together at one end. Do this again to make two bundles of paper.

2

Staple both of the paper bundles together making sure the shortest lengths are on the outside.

3

Fold the strips of paper on one side half down towards the stapled end of the bundles. Line the edges up and staple the strips to the bundle.

4

Repeat on the other side to make the heart shape and staple to fix in place.

5

Make three hearts in total. Attach a short piece of cotton to the top of each heart with sticky tape. Stick them all together to make a string of hearts, ready to hang.

Shoebox Swamp

You will need:
The base of an old shoebox
Paint
Paintbrush
Coloured paper or card
Scissors
Black felt-tip pen
Glue

Transform an old shoebox into a super swamp filled with overhanging trees, lily pads and a hopping frog.

1 Paint your shoe box. Paint green on the bottom and blue on the top, sides and outside.

2 Using different shades of green paper, cut out a wavy shape for some hills and a spiky shape for the grass.

3

Using other coloured paper, cut out a pond, lily pads, clouds, trees, reeds and flowers.

Try creating different scenes, such as a planet-filled outer space theme with zooming rockets.

4

Glue the pond, hills and clouds in first. Then stick the trees on the side.

5

Cut out a shape of a frog from some green card. Draw the frog's features using a black felt-tip pen. Add the frog to your scene along with any other small details such as flowers and reeds. Your scene is complete!

Fruity Fridge Magnets

You will need:
Kitchen foil
Tissue paper
PVA glue
Paintbrush
Black felt-tip pen
Magnets
Double-sided sticky tape

Foil is a great material to mould into any shape. Make any fridge magnets you like. Why not try some letters or numbers?

Decorate the outside of your fridge with these fun food magnets! Use them to attach handy notes to the fridge or to display pieces of art you have just made.

1

Scrunch up a piece of kitchen foil (about 50 cm long) and shape it into a strawberry (which is similar to a heart shape).

2

Cover the whole shape in small pieces of red tissue paper using PVA glue. Leave to dry in a warm place.

3

Draw some pips onto the strawberry using the black felt-tip pen.

4

Cut five leaf shapes with long stems out of green tissue paper. Twist the stems together and glue them on top of the strawberry.

5

Using double-sided tape or glue, stick a magnet to the back of the strawberry. When it is dry you can use it to stick to a fridge or any metal surface.

Tissue Paper Sunlight Catchers

You will need:
Plastic pocket
Tissue paper
PVA glue
Black felt-tip pen
Scissors
Hole punch
Cotton thread

Make your very own stained glass sunlight catchers that will twinkle and sparkle in the light.

1 Cut lots of different shapes out of tissue paper, or rip some into small squares.

2 Glue them onto a plastic pocket in a random pattern using the PVA glue. Leave to dry in a warm place until completely dry. This could take up to 24 hours.

3

Make a template of a star. Draw around this template onto your tissue paper pattern using a black felt-tip pen.

4

Cut out all your shapes. You can cut out just stars, or you could cut out different shapes, too.

5

Stick a length of cotton on top of the stars using sticky tape and hang up!

91

Find Out More

Looking for more ways to have fun with crafts? Here are some ideas...

Fun with Friends

Why not suggest a craft party one day after school? You and your friends could spend the week before collecting interesting materials. Then you can get together one afternoon to share what you have found and make some fantastic crafts. You could even make a joint project, such as a theatre set or doll's house, full of wonderful characters that you can play with afterwards.

Clubs

Does your school have an after school craft club? If so, why not join and show off your skills.

If you are a member of the Brownies or Scouts, you can earn a badge for your brilliant crafts.

Competitions

Why not look out for local competitions that you can enter your crafts into? Many places have summer fêtes with a craft or art competition to enter.

You can also look at using one of your projects to try and win a Blue Peter badge!
www.bbc.co.uk/cbbc/joinin/about-blue-peter-badges

Websites

Here are some crafty websites with great ideas to try:

www.redtedart.com/

www.activityvillage.co.uk/crafts

www.minieco.co.uk/

kids.tate.org.uk/create/

www.nickjr.co.uk/activities/

Books

10 Minute Crafts (Multiple titles), Annalees Lim, Wayland, 2016–2017.

365 Things to Make and Do, Fiona Watt, Usborne, 2007.

51 things to make with Paper Plates, Fiona Hayes, QED, 2017.

Get Into: Sewing, Jane Marland, Wayland, 2016.

I Made That: The Kids' Big Book of Craft Ideas, Susannah Blake, Wayland, 2015.

Paper, Print, Stamp: 50 fun art projects to make, Susie Brooks, Wren & Rook, 2017.

Pop-Out Stencil Art: Dinosaurs, Laura Hambleton, QED Publishing, 2016.

Red Ted Art, Margarita Woodley, Square Peg, 2013.

Glossary

beak the hard part of a bird's mouth

blunt not sharp

concertina a shape made by folding paper backwards and forwards

ellipse a shape that looks like a flattened circle

greenhouse a building used to grow plants all year long. They usually have a glass roof and glass walls.

inspiration an idea that encourages you to do or make something

keepsake box a box where you can keep things that are special to you

magnet a metal material that sticks to other metal materials

mane the long hair around a lion's neck

masterpiece a fantastic piece of artwork

minibeast a small animal such as a bee, ladybird, beetle or spider

mosaic a picture made from lots of smaller bits of paper, tiling or glass

nurture to encourage the growth of plants by watching and watering them when necessary

paper chains decorations made by joining pieces of paper together

paper weight a small heavy object placed on top of papers to stop them moving in the wind or by accident

primary colour red, yellow and blue

secondary colour a colour made by mixing two of the primary colours together

shoot a new growth on a tree or plant

skyline the outline of buildings against sky

stencil a piece of paper or card with a picture that has been cut out, through which paint or pens is drawn onto another piece of paper to make a picture

swamp a very muddy pond or lake

technique a particular way of doing something

template a shape you can draw around again and again to make the same shape

tertiary colour a colour made by mixing a primary and a secondary colour together

texture the feel or look of a surface

tissue paper very thin paper often used as wrapping paper

unique different from everything else

wattle a flap of skin that hangs from the neck of a bird

weaving to make by passing fabric or threads over and under each other

woven a piece of weaving

Index